TECHNOLOGY
IN THE
WORKPLACE™

# WORKING WITH TECH IN
# MANUFACTURING

Rosen
YA™
New York

MARY-LANE KAMBERG

Published in 2021 by The Rosen Publishing Group, Inc.
29 East 21st Street, New York, NY 10010

First Edition

**Library of Congress Cataloging-in-Publication Data**

Names: Kamberg, Mary-Lane, 1948– author.
Title: Working with tech in manufacturing / Mary-Lane Kamberg.
Description: First edition. | New York : Rosen Publishing, 2021.
| Series: Technology in the workplace | Includes bibliographical
references and index.
Identifiers: LCCN 2019018821| ISBN 9781725341654
(library bound) | ISBN 9781725341647 (pbk.)
Subjects: LCSH: Manufacturing industries—Technological innovations—
Juvenile literature. | Employees—Effect of technological innovations on—
Juvenile literature.
Classification: LCC HD9720.5 .K36 2020 | DDC 658.5/14—dc23
LC record available at https://lccn.loc.gov/2019018821

*Printed in China*

# CONTENTS

What if someone rings your doorbell when you're away from home? It might be a friend dropping by. Or it might be a burglar checking to see if the home is ripe to be broken into. The SkyBell HD Wi-Fi Video Doorbell from SkyBell Technologies Inc., based in Southern California, lets you answer the door from a remote location.

This doorbell sends a live, high-definition video alert to a client's smartphone in full color, even at night. Its motion detector turns it on even if the visitor doesn't push the button. The Wi-Fi connection lets the homeowner see, hear, and speak to the person at the door. The device also snaps photos and records live video.

This device uses a technology framework known as the Internet of Things (IoT). IoT systems tie together machines, sensors, and human beings, connecting them via a common network, which incorporates both wired and wireless technologies to help things run smoothly. The technology is one of many consumer products taking advantage of an explosion of technology in this millenium. Although consumers may be familiar with some of these innovations, they may not be aware that manufacturers of these products also use new technology to produce them.

Trends in manufacturing technology include both information technology that helps businesses collect, retrieve, and manipulate data and operational technology, which includes both hardware and software that makes work on the factory floor run efficiently and economically. In addition to IoT, developments include robotics, cloud computing, 3D printing, augmented reality, and nanotechnology.

New information technologies help managers analyze significant data to improve such activities as accounting and long-range planning. Software innovations include manufacturing execution systems (MES), enterprise resource planning (ERP), robotic process automation (RPA), advanced planning and scheduling (APS), and learning management systems (LMS).

Beyond all that, manufacturers also embrace lean and green technologies that reduce waste and minimize the environmental impact of their activities. Many companies have realized lower costs and higher profits from recycling waste, using recycled resources, and reusing wastewater rather than sending it to treatment plants.

With so many developments that encourage automation and that let machines perform tasks that humans once did, some worry that the impact on the workforce will be massive job loss. In fact, in the early 2000s, the United States experienced lost jobs as factories moved overseas in search of cheaper labor and lower corporate taxes. But technology also went a long way to reduce the number of workers needed on the factory floor.

A bottling plant is shown at work here. It is one of many different workplaces that one might encounter if one plans to work in the manufacturing sector.

Other trends are actually working to bring back some factories stateside—that is, back to the United States from abroad. This trend is accompanied by the need for human workers. However, the jobs are not the same as the ones that were lost.

Thanks to innovations, manufacturers need fewer assemblers, fabricators, machinists, and tool and die makers. Instead, today's employers need automation specialists and experts in technology who can design, build, program, monitor, maintain, and repair high-tech machines that work together with humans, rather than replace them. American workers must prepare themselves for the new manufacturing jobs.

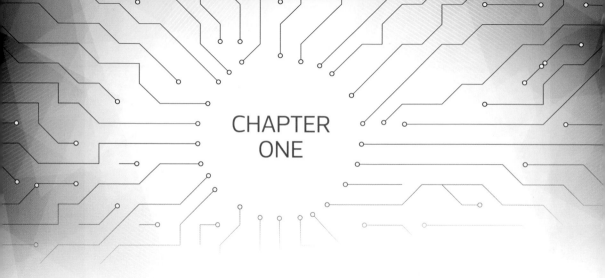

# PUTTING IT ALL TOGETHER

N early all of the items we use in our daily lives are created using the same process: manufacturing. Manufacturing is the process of making items for parts or complete products for sale to customers, whether they are individuals or businesses. Manufacturers use such materials as wood, plastic, metal, rubber, leather, textiles, paper, chemicals, and more to produce goods. Among other areas, manufacturing includes the following industries:

- Clothing and textiles
- Petroleum, chemicals, and plastics
- Electronics, computers, and transportation
- Food production
- Automotive, steel and metal, and cement
- Furniture
- Machinery and power

## THROUGH THE AGES

The process of making things for specific purposes dates to ancient times. Prehistoric cave art discovered in Lascaux, France, that dates to 17,000 BCE indicates that someone created a brush to apply the paint. Up to about 4000 BCE, available materials of gold, copper, meteoric iron, flint, wood, bone, ivory, clay, stone, and

Simple tools have been used for many thousands of years in the manufacture of needed items. The most common and complex tool used to make things (like the pottery shown here) has been human hands.

natural fibers were used to make tools and household items by hand.

As humans made use of new materials and developed new methods, they were able to produce more items at better levels of quality. However, such processes required hours of manual, often skilled labor. Individual artisans made products by hand in small batches. Artisans during the time of the Roman Empire (500 BCE to 476 CE) even mass-produced glass to an extent. Still, the methods used relied on manpower, and production remained slow.

## THE MARCH OF PROGRESS

Individual craftspeople making things by hand was the way most items were made through the nineteenth century. However, the discovery of the Terra-Cotta Army in 1974 proved that assembly-line-style manufacturing existed in ancient times.

In 1974, farmers digging a well in Hi'an, Shaanxi Province, China, discovered a burial pit. It turned out to be the first of three they found. The pits contained life-size terra-cotta sculptures of 8,000 spies, cavalry, and foot soldiers. These were representations of the actual battalions of the Chinese army from many years earlier. Each had clothing and a hairstyle that depicted the fashion of the time and the person's social status. In addition, the scuptures included 150 cavalry horses and 139 bronze chariots with 520 horses.

Groups of 720,000 specialized workers molded interchangeable legs, arms, torsos, and heads by hand. The parts were then assembled, fired in kilns, and painted. A kiln is an oven used to heat to harden clay.

The funeral art was buried near the tomb of Qin Shi Huang. His armies united China at the end of the Warring States Period 478–221 BCE). He was China's first emperor 210–209 BCE). During the previous Shang and Zhou dynasties, human sacrifices of soldiers, attendants, and officials were buried with their leaders to serve the same purpose: protecting the leader in the afterlife.

The first Industrial Revolution began in England in the 1750s and spread to the United States by the nineteenth century. It was a time when inventors created machines that could then themselves make parts with more precision and speed than humans could do alone. Automation was beginning to take hold.

In some cases, mechanization allowed manufacturers to make things more cheaply. For example, textiles made with hand-spun wool cost more than new ones made from cotton spun on a spinning wheel and threaded through a loom. Such processes greatly reduced production time. The lower selling prices of the finished products increased demand.

In hopes of making even more money, manufacturers increased the hours their factories operated and

Workers at a garment factory around 1890 in Schenectady, New York, are shown at their sewing machines. American workers faced harsh work conditions in the nineteenth century, and many still do.

demanded more from workers. Working conditions were often bad. In many places, many children also worked alongside older people. By 1833, the first of several Factory Acts in England restricted hours children could work and set industry standards for child welfare and working conditions.

## THE MACHINE AGE DAWNS

One of the most important engineering developments during the Industrial Revolution was the idea of using interchangeable parts (even though evidence of the use of interchangeable parts dates at least to the Terra-Cotta Army). Interchangeable parts are designed to work in all products of the same kind.

However, before manufacturers adopted this idea widely, parts were specifically designed and made for a particular item. Repairs required individual attention from a skilled craftsman. For example, if the flintlock of a musket failed, a gunsmith had to design and craft a new one for that particular gun. Repairs on many items could be costly and time-consuming.

Using interchangeable parts made with precise machinery, however, meant that unskilled workers could make more products faster at a lower cost than before. If part of the product later broke, an identical part could easily and quickly replace it.

Eli Whitney, who invented the cotton gin, is sometimes credited with coming up with the concept of interchangeable parts. This reputation arose from Whitney's factory that produced 15,000 high-quality muskets for the US government. The muskets were the first guns manufactured with machine-made, interchangeable parts.

Whitney was just one of several manufacturers of his era who made such innovations. In the early 1700s, Swedish clockmaker Christopher Polhem made clock gears using uniform parts that could be used in different clocks. In France, Honoré LeBlanc proposed the use of standardized patterns for firearm parts. Two English naval engineers, Samuel Bentham and Marc Brunel, produced wooden pulleys for sailing ships. Throughout the nineteenth century, factories replaced individual workshops, and machines took over many jobs.

In addition to using interchangeable parts, engineers Bentham and Brunel also made innovations in the division of labor on the manufacturing floor. This division referred to who did what tasks to complete a product's manufacture. Instead of a single craftsman making an entire item, workers perform only one task in the process. A modern example is a worker at a car assembly plant who paints the front passenger side door of a sedan. Others paint the other doors, while a whole different set of workers installs the engine.

## WORKIN' THE LINE

By the early twentieth century, another innovation revolutionized production. Ransom E. Olds created the first assembly line for automobile production in 1901. His Oldsmobile Company used the method to mass-produce the Oldsmobile Model R Curved Dash Runabout. An assembly line takes the division of labor and breaks it down to small, concrete steps. It is a step-by-step manufacturing method where workers and machines complete a sequence of simple steps as the semifinished item moves along to the next workstation. An assembly line is sometimes called a production line. Employees who work on assembly lines are called line workers.

# WHITNEY'S GAMBLE

In 1797, the US government expected to go to war with France. It approved $800,000 to purchase weapons that included muskets fashioned after the 1763 French Charleville model. At the time, Eli Whitney was almost bankrupt. His 1793 invention of the cotton gin had revolutionized planting in the United States but failed to produce a profit.

Whitney had no experience making guns. Still, he won a twenty-eight-month $134,000 government contract for 10,000 muskets. He built and equipped a factory to make guns with interchangeable parts in New Haven, Connecticut. But he failed to produce a single weapon by January 1801. Government officials called him to Washington, D.C., to account for his use of federal funds.

The inventor decided to prove himself—and to justify a contract extension and further funding for his venture. Whitney took ten muskets into the US Congress. He broke them down and scrambled the parts. He then reassembled the muskets, using apparently random components. The demonstration worked. Congress enthusiastically extended his contract, and the first of the muskets were delivered three months later.

Although the engineering process was sound, the demonstration was not. The parts Whitney used were not actually interchangeable. He had secretly marked the components so he could easily reassemble the guns.

Then, in 1913, Henry Ford added a conveyor belt to an assembly line. Now, a Model T under construction moved along to eighty-four different workstations. Each station performed only one step. He called using interchangeable parts with a moving conveyor system flow production.

The innovation at Ford's factory cut down production time dramatically. Ford's line workers could finish a car in two hours and thirty minutes, compared to the twelve hours it took before. A year later, Ford had whittled the

This 1915 image shows workers busy on the production line making Model T cars at a Ford Motors factory. Ford and other industry leaders revolutionized not just the cars they made, but how they made them.

process down to only ninety-three minutes. Savings on time and labor meant Ford could build cars at a lower cost, with a resulting lower price to consumers. Meanwhile, demand for automobiles was increasing.

## THE BIG DEAL

During World War II, when the Japanese attacked Pearl Harbor, Hawaii, on December 7, 1941, President Franklin Roosevelt addressed the US Congress to ask them to declare war. Roosevelt also realized the nation needed badly to ramp up its industrial production to win the war. He said America's enemies must be "out-fought and out-produced overwhelmingly so that there can be no question of our ability to provide a crushing superiority of equipment in any theatre of the world war."

He set challenging two-year goals for the production of 185,000 aircraft, 120,000 tanks, and 55,000 antiaircraft guns. In response, defense contractors expanded operations. Automobile factories and other manufacturers switched production to car, truck, and aircraft engines; aircraft fuselages; and 1,550,000 parts for B-24 Liberator long-range bombers.

Many factories stayed open around the clock, using the moving assembly line process and interchangeable parts. They produced war goods faster and on a larger scale than ever before. At the same time, quality remained a top priority so no American lives would be lost to faulty equipment.

The war stimulated economic activity that brought the nation out of the Great Depression. A few years after the war, consumers were ready and eager to buy cars, televisions, and household appliances. The demand stimulated manufacturers to use lessons learned during the war to increase the supply of domestic goods at reasonable cost.

In 1960, 24 percent of America's workforce worked in manufacturing, according to the US Bureau of Labor Statistics (BLS). From the people who researched and designed new products, to the engineers who figured out how to create machines to produce them and the line workers on the factory floor, the manufacturing sector supported a wide range of occupations.

Assemblers and fabricators, for example, assembled parts as well as finished products using tools, machines, and their own hands. Machinists and tool and die makers produced precision metal parts, instruments, and tools. Metal and plastic machine workers cut, shaped, and formed metal and plastic materials or pieces. Other workers painted or coated such products as cars, jewelry, and ceramics. Welders, cutters, solderers, and brazers cut or joined metal parts. Finally, quality-control inspectors checked products to make sure they were made properly and complied with applicable laws and regulations.

Toward the end of the twentieth century, however, American manufacturing changed dramatically. Due to many factors, including high oil and energy costs, profits

A woman adjusts a part on a microwave oven at a factory in Port Klang, Malaysia, in 1998. By the 1990s, increasing numbers of jobs went overseas because companies didn't want to pay higher wages in the United States.

began to fall. The well-paid jobs that the manufacturing sector brought with it began to taper off, and eventually started to disappear. Corporations sought cheaper labor overseas, often at much lower wages.

To slash their expenses, corporations moved production jobs overseas to Asia and Central and South America. Workers could be found in places like China, Bangladesh, Thailand, and elsewhere that would do more work for a tiny fraction of the wages that Western workers were accustomed to. Machines were beginning to replace human workers, and new technologies would alter the factory floor once again.

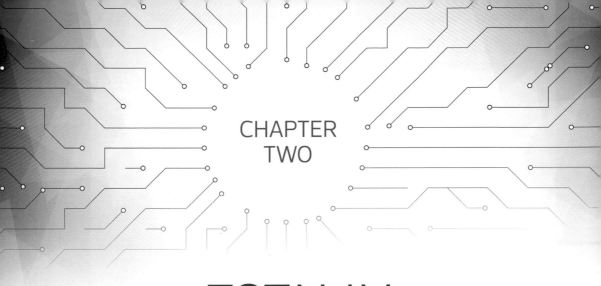

# TOTALLY AUTOMATIC

If you walk into the Changying Precision Technology Company in Dongguan, China, on a typical business day, you might think the facility is closed. There's no one around. But the factory is humming twenty-four hours a day. With robotic assistance, the few human employees remaining each produce around 21,000 cell phone components per month. That number used to be closer to just 8,000 each. It's not because the humans are working harder; there are not that many left doing the work.

First reported in 2015, the company replaced nearly 600 human employees with 60 robotic arms that work on 10 production lines. The company also automated machining equipment, transport trucks, and other machines. In addition to higher productivity, the occurrence of product defects decreased from about 25 percent to less than 5 percent. The humans who remained

Examine a random zipper on any garment or accessory you own, and chances are it could have been made at this YKK plant, the largest zipper factory in the world, located in Tuen Mun, in China's Hong Kong region.

on the job were tasked with monitoring the production lines and computer control system.

## CHANGING TIMES

Robotics is changing manufacturing and has been doing so for a long time. The first industrial robots performed assembly-line operations. However, as they became capable of more tasks, new uses came to be explored.

Manufacturers use the machines in warehouses, where they navigate complex floor plans faster and more safely than human workers.

Automotive factories are also expanding robot use beyond the assembly line. The new machines are easy to modify to accommodate whatever tools are needed. And because some operate on compressed air, they're easy to adapt for tasks beyond simply putting parts together. In the woodworking industry, robots plane wood, build pallets, and cut lumber to particular specifications.

Some robots work alone, replacing what humans would otherwise do on assembly lines. But a new generation of collaborative robots—called cobots—are designed to work alongside human employees. The robots handle the harder, more boring, or more dangerous tasks, while living workers control the machines.

# INDUSTRIAL ROBOTICS TIMELINE

1480 – Leonardo da Vinci draws sketches of robotic arms and humanlike robots in his notebook. The devices use pulleys, weights, and gears like clocks.
1950 – Isaac Asimov publishes *I, Robot*.

*(continued on the next page)*

*(continued from the previous page)*

1954 – Inspired by Asimov's book, Joseph Engelberger and George Devol file for a patent for a mechanical arm and build the Unimate, the first industrial robot.

1961 – General Motors buys 450 Unimates to stack hot, die-cast metal parts.

1969 – Victor Scheinman creates the first electric, computer-controlled robot arm. In 1974, the updated Stanford Arm can assemble a Ford Model-T water pump.

1970s – Innovations include the use of electromagnets instead of hydraulics and the inventions of programmable robots and robots controlled by microprocessors.

1980s – New robot arms use compressed air instead of hydraulics or electricity.

2000 – Honda introduces its humanoid robot, ASIMO, to coexist with humans. The 2014 version can use sign language.

2009 – Universal Robots introduces the UR5, a collaborative robot or "cobot," designed to work alongside humans.

2012 – The International Federation of Robotics estimates the worldwide population of robots at 1,235,000.

2013 to present – Technology continues to improve the efficiency and effectiveness of industrial robots with more sophistication.

## BEYOND ROBOTS

Robotics is an example of operational technology. This category of tech includes both hardware and software that control or monitor automated machinery. Information

Older machines, like the olive press used by these Italians in the 1980s, often need a great deal of human guidance and operation. Newer machines and technologies require less human oversight.

technology is another category that includes computers that connect all the different parts of a business or company together.

In addition to robotics, other operational technologies affect the ways businesses make things. The Internet of Things (IoT) is closely related to robotics. It involves machines, sensors, and humans working together and is controlled using wireless connectivity. With

IoT, computing devices placed in objects send and receive information via the internet. The devices can communicate with a network without human input.

The actual things that can be integrated into an IoT system include toys, lamps, headphones, smartwatches, fitness bands, coffee makers, motion sensors, smart thermostats, washing machines, and driverless vehicles. Even jet engines use IoT, where thousands of sensors can now collect and send data to ensure efficient operation. So do drills on oil rigs.

## TALKING TO EACH OTHER

Although modern uses of IoT now include devices for homes and offices, some earlier applications were known as M2M, or "machine-to-machine" systems. In general, IoT now connects people to people, people to things, and things to things. IoT results in better communication, faster response times, and greater efficiency.

The ideas for IoT have been around in science fiction for a long time. By the 1980s, people started to believe IoT was an idea whose time had come. However, the necessary technology was not yet available. The inexpensive sensors and energy-efficient processors that could connect to a worldwide web were still in the not-so-distant future. Such tools didn't become cost effective to roll out commercially until the twenty-first century. Now, low-power chips that can communicate wirelessly, along with more broadband internet availability and

A large control room must be manned at this industrial bakery. Sensors, cameras, and other tools throughout the facility beam back the real-time, up-to-date information managers need to run a business like this daily.

increased cellular and wireless networking have made IoT practical.

The goal of IoT is to make things more efficient for the customers using it. Professionals in the health care and transportation industries and workers at utilities are using IoT devices to collect data about their operations. However, IoT's most widespread application by far is in the manufacturing sector. Manufacturers add sensors to parts of their products. These sensors transmit information about the components' efficiency. This lets the companies know when a part is likely to fail. That way, a new part can replace the old one before it causes damage. Companies also use data from IoT sensors to improve efficiencies in their supply chains.

IoT systems are proliferating. In 2016, Cisco Systems, Inc., a large, long-standing networking and information technology pioneer, estimated that number of connected devices globally to be about fifteen billion. It predicted the number to increase to fifty billion by 2020. The microchip producer Intel predicts that that number will be much higher. The company expects that more than 200 billion IoT products would be in use by then. Research firm IDC Technologies said worldwide spending on IoT devices and services would reach $1.7 trillion by 2020.

## WALKING ON A CLOUD

Data transmitted by so many IoT devices creates a huge amount of data. Businesses are using cloud computing for their data processing. Cloud computing is the use of remote servers to store, manage, and process data on an internet network instead of a personal computer or a company's on-site information system.

When an IoT device connects to another to send data using the internet, IoT platforms serve as the bridge between the devices that collect information and the data network where it is used. In information technology, a platform is hardware and software that hosts a service. Some key platforms include Amazon Web Services, Microsoft Azure, ThingWorx IoT Platform, IBM's Watson, Cisco IoT Cloud Connect, Salesforce IoT Cloud, Oracle Integration Cloud, and GE Predix.

At first, manufacturers hesitated to use cloud computing due to concerns about connectivity and security. However, computer scientists are working on those limitations, and manufacturers are coming on board. One benefit to using the cloud in manufacturing includes the ability to share data across multiple sites, including factories. It also helps reduce costs and production time and improve product quality and consistency among different plants. In short, cloud computing reduces information technology costs. It also augments the powers of existing hardware and software.

## ADD-ONS

First conceived in 1980 and first patented in 1986, 3D printing continues to present opportunities for manufacturing. The process, also called additive manufacturing, is a process for creating a physical object, starting with a plan created with computer-aided design software (CAD). A 3D printer then adds

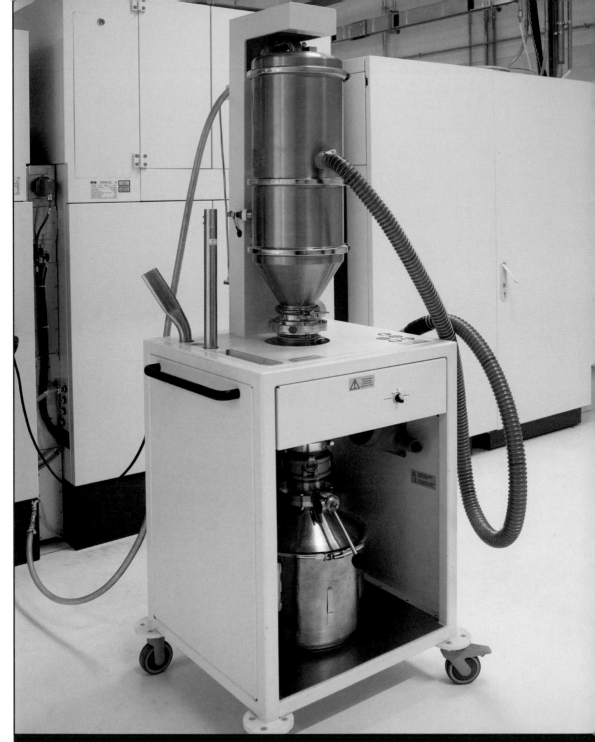

This metal unit is actually a 3D printer. Such printers might become integral to making prototypes and one-off samples of future products, and may even become a major part of the manufacturing sector itself.

a sequence of thin layers or slices of material to make the item. The final step is a finishing process, such as sanding, painting, or lacquering.

Advanced 3D printing can help reduce the time needed to create a prototype, or first example, of a product. Complex shapes and interlocking parts made this way need little or no complex assembly. Manufacturers can also produce small quantities of special orders quickly and cheaply without specialized tools.

Using 3D printing helps companies reduce the waste identified with other techniques. For example, most production cuts away from a block of material to create an object. The material removed is wasted. However, 3D printing simply adds what's needed a little at a time, so more of the original material ends up in the finished product.

Among many other applications, 3D printing has been used for hearing aids, dental appliances, jewelry, and parts for the aerospace industry. Materials that can be used in 3D printing include wax, sand, glass, foods, plastics, ceramics, resins, metals, textiles, and even human tissue. In 2015, the National Aeronautics and Space Administration (NASA), the nation's agency in charge of space exploration and study, used alloys for 3D printing for the first time. Manufacturers have moved beyond simply using 3D printing for prototypes. They are now producing working parts and entire products, such as robotic arms, bone replacements, and even building blocks for affordable housing.

# THE FINAL FRONTIER

NASA uses 3D printing to manufacture parts for space vehicles. So does a relatively new entrant into space: the aerospace technology and travel company SpaceX. In 2014, SpaceX launched a Falcon 9 rocket that had a 3D-printed main oxidizer valve body in one of its engines. The part worked well in the face of high vibration, high-pressure liquid oxygen, and temperatures between -238 degrees F (-150 degrees C) and -460 degrees F (-273 degrees C), according to the company's website. The printed valve had superior strength, ductility, and fracture resistance than a part cast the traditional way.

Also in 2014, NASA used a 3D printer to manufacture a mirror mount using several different alloys. Using more than one alloy in a single object had been impossible prior to NASA's innovation. In addition, NASA worked with Made in Space Inc. to create a 3D printer that a SpaceX resupply mission delivered to the International Space Station. It was the first step toward a machine shop in space that could let astronauts make tools and parts onboard. Since then, astronauts aboard the station successfully printed an engraved faceplate to demonstrate the technology.

## EXPANDING REALITY

If you were one of the millions of users in 2016 who wandered their neighborhoods trying to catch their favorite Pokemon by looking at superimposed images on your phone, you have direct experience with augmented reality (AR) technology.

AR is an interactive experience that enhances a user's view of the real world by adding a computer-generated image, often seen in specialized eyewear. Although you might associate AR with fun and games, businesses are using it, too. For instance, furniture retailer IKEA uses the technology to let customers see how its products will look in the customers' homes.

AR is still a young technology, but manufacturers are finding important ways to use it. For example, AR assists workers wearing special helmets or eyewear with complex assembly tasks. Work instructions are available through hands-free, voice-controlled devices that show work instructions and technical drawings in the worker's line of sight.

Instructions for maintenance of manufacturing equipment can also be displayed using AR. Steps for inspections can be shown, and workers can speak their inspection results instead of submitting written reports. The technology also enhances quality assurance by preventing errors and highlighting features that don't meet required specifications.

If additional support is needed, AR lets workers interact with experts at remote locations. The experts can see what the worker sees and offer advice without traveling to the work site. AR saves companies money on training employees, too. Training takes less time when images of training information are superimposed on the actual parts involved, so tasks are easier to learn.

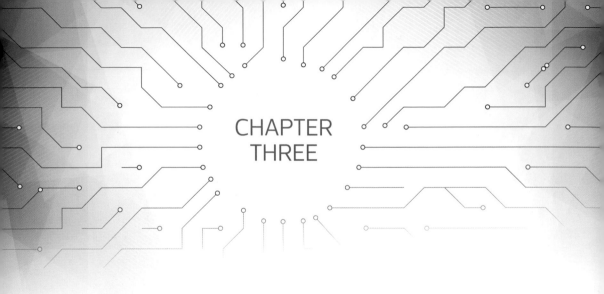

# THE SOFTER SIDE

A long with adopting operational technology, manufacturers are embracing information technology in the form of software for manufacturing execution systems (MES), enterprise resource planning (ERP), robotic process automation (RPA), advanced planning and scheduling (APS), and learning management systems (LMS).

MES keeps track of what's happening on the factory floor. That includes whatever humans, machines, and robots are doing. MES collects accurate data in real time to ensure that manufacturing operations work effectively. It also manages documents. Beyond simply collecting information and managing documents, however, MES actually controls the activities on the factory floor, including scheduling, maintenance, and quality control. The system helps shop floor supervisors react quickly and make faster

Efficient warehousing and storage protocols are also part of the industrial process. Manufactured items, whatever they are, need to be stored, moved, distributed, and sold.

decisions about such issues as machine breakdowns, maintenance times, and employee absenteeism.

This ability leads to production efficiency that keeps costs as low as possible while ensuring product quality. It helps companies use resources wisely, improve the speed of production, reduce waste, and comply with industry standards and regulations. Examples of MES software include Factory Logix, IQMS, EZ-MES, Prodsmart, and Fishbowl.

## WORKING TOGETHER

Along with MES software, many manufacturers are using ERP software to manage the flow of data for accounting, purchasing, and project management. ERP allows readily available access to accurate information for all of a company's departments, using the same database. It also prevents duplication of activities by more than one area. This improves decision-making as well as planning for the future.

ERP is flexible and can be adapted with additional features as a manufacturer's needs change. This type of software not only increases communication within a company, it can improve communication with suppliers, customers, and others outside the company.

Using such software helps companies stay on top of changing government regulations and ensure that the company complies with required financial records and data security. For example, publicly traded companies are required to keep records that are 100 percent accurate. ERP ensures that the record-keeping system follows official, generally accepted accounting principles. Security features built into the programs have advanced user-approval methods to protect data from theft and corporate espionage.

Manufacturers of foodstuffs must be able to trace their goods throughout the manufacturing process in case of mishandling or contamination. ERP lets companies find the source of trouble, including knowing which plant is involved, to quickly remedy such situations. Companies can choose from a wide range of ERP providers. Some of the better-known ones include Microsoft Dynamics NAV, ShopEdge ERP, Indigo, Cyframe, and Base2.

## ROBOTS 'R US

Robotic process automation (RPA) takes manufacturing tasks out of the hands of humans and assigns them to robots instead. The technology is based on the idea of

Film techs work on a robotic arm, part of James Cameron's 2003 underwater documentary, *Ghosts of the Abyss*. Such equipment might be tailored for use in underwater manufacturing and production processes.

artificial intelligence. Artificial intelligence is a branch of computer science that lets machines work and react like humans. The software gives machines the ability to see, recognize speech, learn, plan, translate languages, and even make decisions.

The automation programs robots and other machines to perform dull, repetitive jobs humans once did. It improves accuracy and cuts the required production time, resulting in savings for the company. The technology handles such "office jobs" as accounting, data entry, customer service, purchase order issuing, and the creation of online access credentials. RPA suppliers include Automation Anywhere, UiPath, Blue Prism, Pegasystems, Antworks, NICE, and Kofax Kapow.

## WHAT? HOW? WHO? WHEN? WHAT IF?

The efficient and profitable manufacture of cars, clocks, or jet aircraft requires significant planning and coordination of materials, workers, and shop floor availability. Planning includes deciding what will be done, how it will be done, and how long it will take. Planning also includes both short-term and long-term targets. Plans must be detailed, and time estimates must be accurate for a factory's efficient operation.

Planners break down the entire production process into individual tasks in a logical sequence or chronological order. They must take into account which resources will be needed. Once a plan is in place, scheduling determines who will do the jobs on which dates and times. Traditionally, planning and scheduling depended on manual procedures to create step-by-step instructions and to schedule the work.

However, a manual system can be slow and unmanageable, especially if something disrupts the plan. For example, what if parts ordered from an outside source fail to arrive on time? What if a machine breaks down? How easy will it be to adjust the plan and schedule?

Today, advanced planning and scheduling (APS) software, some of which operates in a cloud environment, simplifies planning and scheduling for manufacturers. Some APS suppliers include Prodsmart, Realtrac, E2 Shop System, and Royal4 Enterprise.

## LEARNING CURVES

As technology continues to add new ways to increase productivity and cut costs, human workers must learn how to design, program, monitor, operate, control, maintain, and troubleshoot robots and machinery. One more information technology trend is a learning management system (LMS). This software evolved from e-learning, lessons available through electronic media, often online. LMS can administer, document, track, and report on a manufacturer's education, job training, or professional development activities.

Before LMS software became available, manufacturers with multiple locations had to print hard copies of training materials. They also had to pay travel expenses for instructors and perhaps rent training site space.

Gigantic machines once existed only in big science-fiction films, like 2017's *Star Wars: The Last Jedi.* Giant, large-scale automated manufacturing projects might be the rule and not the exception in the coming century, however.

Employees and trainees had to attend lengthy meetings at particular times and places.

An LMS centralizes the training process, especially if it's a cloud-based system. All the information and training materials are available online and stored on a remote server to reduce the risk of loss. As information changes, it's easy to update materials for new trends, scientific evidence, or changes in government regulations.

Trainees can access information from anywhere at any time with a smartphone or tablet. They can learn at their own pace and review material as needed, and don't have to wait for the next class. It's also easy for the company to include links to Facebook, Twitter, LinkedIn, and online forums so their employees can connect with other employees with similar roles. In addition, companies using LMS can easily track trainees' progress to see if they need additional help to understand a concept or complete performance guidelines.

# BUILDING BRIDGES

One example of an LMS system is the Universal Robots Academy, from Universal Robots, headquartered in Odense, Denmark. The goal is to bridge the skills gap in manufacturing and improve robot literacy worldwide by teaching people how to program robots. Cobots working on an assembly line, for instance, perform routine jobs while freeing up human workers to perform more complex tasks. That way the robots work with humans, not replace them.

But first, people need to know how to program these collaborative robots to adapt them for particular uses. The Universal Robots Academy is an online learning service that teaches how to program robots. The eighty-seven-minute course covers creating basic programs. It also teaches how to order a robot's end effector to perform a designated job. An end effector is the object at the end of a robotic arm that performs the desired tasks. The course also covers connecting inputs and outputs that let a machine receive and send data as well as how to apply safety features.

The course, which is available in English, Spanish, German, French, and Chinese, is available free to the general public. Universal Robots officials hope the learning system encourages the use of cobots and helps increase the market for its robot arms.

## THE LITTLE THINGS

What if manufacturers could make products from the atomic level up? That's the idea behind nanotechnology. Nanotechnology is the manipulation of tiny matter: atoms and molecules. With this technology, scientists could create such elements as carbon, nitrogen, and oxygen for manufacturers' use as raw materials. Instead of using resources that require mining and processing, these businesses could reduce the cost of making end products.

By manipulating matter, nanotechnology creates the ability to develop new materials that last longer or have desired properties, like greater strength or lighter weight. This may sound like science fiction. However, according to the Society of Toxicology, new materials developed this way are in current use.

A composite made of clay nanoparticles is 200 times stronger and 5 times more flexible than steel. It also increases copper's electrical conductivity five-fold. And it makes aluminum half as dense. This material keeps products from rusting or changing with temperature fluctuations. When used in tennis racket frames, the greater strength gives the player better power and control when hitting the ball. The composite makes the shafts of golf clubs more uniform, which improves the player's swing. The nanoparticles also make high-end tennis balls and golf balls last longer.

The Project on Emerging Nanotechnologies at the Virginia Polytechnic Institute and State University, commonly known as Virginia Tech, identifies more than 1,790 such products already on the market. The list includes cotton sheets, degreasers, pain relievers, and cosmetics.

## LIVING IN A MATERIAL WORLD

Interest in nanotechnology has increased interest in materials science and engineering. Researchers in this field include those with specialties in applied physics and chemistry, as well as chemical, mechanical, civil, and electrical engineering. They seek to understand the atomic structure and composition of materials compared with their properties as well as learning how to synthesize or change them.

Goals of the science include the ability to select resources for production and to create new materials with such desired characteristics as strength, lighter weight, flexibility, electrical conductivity, resistance to temperature changes, and more. The field is of particular interest to manufacturers who use metals, ceramics, and rubber as well as those who produce paint and other coatings. It also holds potential for such industries as energy, ground transportation, aerospace, computers, communications, and medicine.

The explosion of interest in materials science prompted the Lawrence Berkeley National Laboratory in Berkeley, California, to create the Materials Project. The lab falls under the jurisdiction of the US Department of Energy Office of Science. It's managed by the University of California. The Materials Project is a huge online database

Other kinds of factories manufacture textiles, like this plant does. Textiles—any kind of cloth or woven fabric—are used in further manufacturing clothing, furniture, and other consumer goods.

open to anyone. Its aim is to accelerate materials research and innovation.

The database includes information on structure and properties of known materials. Its high-performance, fast supercomputing abilities also allow researchers to predict traits of new materials.

## THE NEXT STEP

Nanotechnology paves the way for a new development in production: atomically precise manufacturing (APM). This process arranges each atom in a specific location among other atoms to make raw materials, structures, devices, and end products. APM eliminates defects caused by missing or extra atoms or impurities from the presence of the wrong atoms.

Molecular machines already exist. They're used in biochemical research with the intention of use in medicines and health care. Another potential use of the technology is the development of very strong materials for military use and lightweight materials for use in transportation. Nanomaterials also present possibilities for greater speed and efficiency in computer technology.

# TECHNOLOGY AT WORK

Manufacturers are embracing new technologies. For example, mobile and AR technologies affect the entire manufacturing process from design to the factory floor. In some lower-skilled jobs, mobile technology helps workers in receiving departments. They used to have to manually count and inspect boxes of supplies that arrived at the dock. They then compared the delivery to the purchase order to be sure everything arrived. They also filled out paperwork needed to record the shipment. That information was then inserted into the companies' inventory records.

Instead of relying on manual methods, the workers can perform the task faster and more easily and accurately with a mobile app for automatic shipping notification. They log in and use a finger scanner to check containers for shipper numbers. The app verifies

Even the process of using forklifts to move merchandise, like this worker moving juice in a bottling plant, might become completely automated in the next decade or two.

what has been received and automatically updates the factory's inventory.

In the warehouse, forklift operators can use a tablet mounted on their machines to help move materials. They use handheld scanners to read barcodes that indicate where the goods should be stored. By pushing the Put button, the workers accurately put away each container and move on to the next. In both cases, information is recorded in real time, so managers can keep tabs on up-to-the-minute developments.

## SEEING IS BELIEVING

With augmented reality eyeglasses or helmets, workers can easily find parts in a well-stocked warehouse. A needed part is highlighted on the field of vision and tells the worker where to find it. When the worker arrives at the proper shelf, the AR display marks a colored square on the proper bin. The part is located quickly and accurately.

On an automaker's assembly line, AR shows workers not only which parts go where, but also the order the parts are to be assembled. In training, AR replaces manual instructions and acts as an individual instructor for each trainee, showing the exact steps needed to accomplish such tasks as assembly, maintenance, and inspection.

Technology is changing the way production workers do their jobs. That means workers must change, too. According to the US Bureau of Labor Statistics in 2018, such traditional production jobs as fabricator, assembler, machinist, and quality control inspector are in the process of being replaced by machines. These jobs traditionally offered good pay for workers without college degrees. Now, however, the manufacturing workforce must adapt to survive.

The good news is advances in technology let machines perform jobs that are too dangerous or even impossible for humans. These developments open new roles for different kinds of workers: designers, builders, managers, and people to program, monitor,

# SMART HARD HATS

Before augmented reality products existed, workers at noisy steel plants had trouble communicating with each other to gather information. The work areas were too loud to yell or use walkie-talkies. When work stopped or started, operators had to leave their stations to get data in a quieter control room. The extra time needed to do that decreased productivity.

Today, however, a wearable, hands-free device like the DAQRI smart helmet combines the features of a traditional industrial hard hat with an IoT device equipped with augmented reality, depth sensors, cameras, and more. The helmet connects humans and machines with such information as photographs, videos, thermal and environmental noise monitoring, and 3D mapping right on the work floor.

Simply eliminating trips to the control room increases productivity and shortens downtime. Additional benefits include improved worker safety. Temperature readings warn workers of equipment that's too hot to handle. The thermal feature also lets operators "see through walls" with X-ray-like vision to be sure tubes and machines are functioning properly. And sensors tell wearers if they're in danger from such moveable machinery as a forklift coming too close. An Intel sixth generation m7 processor powers the DAQRI smart helmet, which works without Wi-Fi, Bluetooth, or GPS connection.

and maintain robots. Companies also need information technology experts to develop software to manage robots and train workers to perform new factory tasks.

## COME FLY WITH ME

The Boeing Corporation, based in Seattle, Washington, now officially includes 3D printing as part of its standard design process for its airplanes, rotorcraft, rockets, satellites, and missiles. The aerospace giant turned to 3D printing when it noticed a decline in orders for geosynchronous earth orbit (GEO) satellites. A GEO satellite stays in one spot in space in relation to Earth's rotation. This positioning lets the satellite serve the same area even though the planet below is turning.

A technician checks wires and fuses to ensure that all the machines and factory floor equipment are working properly in a facility.

The technology lets the manufacturer remain flexible to meet the changing needs of the marketplace. It allows faster, cost-effective production while also offering options for complex designs. For example, Boeing's SES-15 satellite provides Wi-Fi access to passengers on flights above North and Central America. 3D printing was used to make more than fifty metal parts for the satellite.

## STAYING LEAN

Lean manufacturing aims to reduce wasted time as well as materials. Japanese automaker Toyota introduced the idea of lean manufacturing in the early 1990s. Technologies associated with lean manufacturing include meters and sensors that monitor, control, and reduce waste.

Lean manufacturers use operational and information technology to identify and reduce or eliminate several types of waste, not just solid materials. The also try to eliminate product defects, overproduction, wait times, unused talent, transportation inefficiency, and more.

Toyota also embraced green manufacturing, which refers to environmentally friendly practices. The company has since set a goal of operating sustainable plants. According to its definition, a sustainable factory should be able to run for more than a century with very little enviromental impact. To achieve this goal, Toyota strives to use such renewable energy as solar and wind power. And it works to preserve the natural environment with conservation activities like tree planting.

# STRIVING FOR PERFECTION

A business strategy first developed in 1980 has taken on new meaning in light of lean manufacturing processes. Bill Smith, an engineer at Motorola, introduced Six Sigma as a set of methods to improve production. A business that adopts the plan sets a goal to analyze data and use the information to reduce the number of variations from customer specifications to 3.4 per million chances to create a defect. In short, the goal is to approach perfection.

The basic ideas encourage management and employee teams to understand the work process, reduce waste, lower costs, increase profits, and improve the customer experience. Six Sigma companies focus on what their customers need and want. According to the plan, use of every resource must create value for the end customer. If not, it should be eliminated. Advanced measurements and statistics help companies identify potential problems as well as find ways to improve workflow. Today, lean manufacturing practices have been added to Six Sigma ideas with a focus on cost-saving and waste-reduction measures.

Centrifuges reduce water pollution by limiting the number of solids in wastewater. Catalytic converters reduce air pollution from engine exhaust. Technology also enables the development of alternative chemicals to replace such pollutants as acetone, xylene, and methylene

A wastewater basin is shown here. Many industrial processes end up with surplus gray water and other unwanted materials and liquids, which the law mandates be disposed or stored somehow, and safely.

chloride. Along with helping the environment, these technologies benefit manufacturing businesses as a whole by saving money and increasing employee morale and customer satisfaction.

## GOING GREEN

American telecommunications company Motorola has also adopted ways to establish environmentally friendly operations. These methods recycle materials, moderate emissions, and use fewer natural resources, while improving the quality of their products.

For example, Motorola focuses on green design to improve its products. In 2018, its average phone charger in standby mode used 70 percent less energy than in 2000, according to the company's website, and it used 66 percent less energy than the standard set by the US Environmental Protection Agency. Motorola's Smart Actions app reduced the number of battery charge cycles by one-third compared to previous ones.

To reduce its use of natural resources, Motorola has made use of plastic from recycled water bottles. This also creates a market for used materials. The "reduce, reuse, recycle" theme also applies to its packaging. Motorola has reduced the weight and volume of its packaging and replaced plastic packaging with 100 percent recycled pulp. Recycled pulp is a material made from paper fibers from recycled paper that has had ink removed. Imagine the number of phones sold each year, and the impact of these measures seems evident.

## RIDING THE GREEN BANDWAGON

General Mills, a food manufacturer headquartered in Minneapolis, Minnesota, joined with other manufacturers using green practices. The company once sent its solid waste to a landfill. However, it found that the oat hulls left over from making Cheerios cereal could be burned as fuel. The company now sells the waste to customers who use it for heat.

According to the company website, General Mills recycles or reuses more than 80 percent of its glass, metal, cardboard, plastics, paper, and reusable photocopier cartridges.

MillerCoors Brewing Company, headquartered in Golden, Colorado, annually produces 45 million gallons (170 million liters) of wasted beer. Instead of sending the 9,000 tons (8,164 metric tons) of wastewater to treatment plants, the company turns it into 3 million gallons (11 million l) of ethanol. The ethanol is blended with gasoline and sold through Valero Energy gas stations in Colorado.

## GAINING ACCESS TO ROBOTICS

The use of learning management systems to train new employees as well as update workers on new materials, processes, machines, and regulations has gained wide acceptance among manufacturers. The Whirlpool Corporation, a manufacturer and marketer of home appliances headquartered in Benton Harbor, Michigan,

Ideally, technology in its many forms will contribute to making any factory or facility a positive, collaborative, and supportive working environment at all levels.

was among the first companies to use the Universal Robots Academy (see chapter 3) online LMS. All training on Universal Robots products at the company's Ohio plant uses the system.

Employees learn at their own pace on-site, without having to go elsewhere for basic education. Employees study only the parts that apply to the skills for their particular jobs, so they don't waste time on knowledge they'll never use. The Universal Robots Academy's interactive method makes the learning hands-on and easy for employees to apply to their individual work stations.

## DIAMONDS IN THE ROUGH

A diamond is the hardest-known substance, and drill bits made from industrial diamonds are routinely used to drill through rock. However, one property of the crystal structure is the tendency to split apart—or cleave   due to the weak planes that run through the material. This trait makes is easy for a jeweler to cut facets when the diamond is used as a gemstone. However, it makes it more difficult to use for drilling.

The General Electric Company (GE), a global conglomerate headquartered in Boston, Massachusetts, has interests in aviation, health care, power, renewable energy, the digital industry, additive manufacturing, venture capital and finance, lighting, and oil and gas. GE used nanotechnology to improve the characteristics of diamonds to prevent failure from cleaving when used as drill bits.

The company created Stratapax, a material made from synthetic diamond powder bonded to tungsten-carbide studs and heated below the melting point. The result is an extremely hard drill bit that won't cleave.

# READY OR NOT?

B etween 2000 and 2016, the United States lost more than five million production jobs, according to the news network CNN. More than 51,000 US factories closed between 1998 and 2008, according to *Sending Jobs Overseas: The Cost to America's Economy and Working Families*, a report by Working America and the AFL-CIO.

The decline in traditional manufacturing employment was expected to continue. Although more than twelve million Americans still worked in production, in 2016 the BLS predicted an additional decline of 4 percent between 2016 and 2026 in that sector—approximately 406,900 jobs.

Once the overseas factories opened, suppliers followed, resulting in further US job losses. For efficiency, makers of the hundreds of parts for an iPhone or iPad, for example, need to be close to where the products are assembled. Waiting for shipments of parts from far away can mean loss of production and higher costs.

This long-abandoned plant in Detroit, Michigan, used to make Packard cars. One fear surrounding automation in manufacturing now is more factories closing, leaving even more workers jobless.

## REVERSAL OF FORTUNE?

With the stated goal of reversing a big loss of manufacturing jobs in the United States between 1998 and 2008, President Donald Trump reduced federal regulations and encouraged Congress to reduce corporate taxes to 21 percent starting in 2018 by passing the Tax Cuts and Jobs Act of 2017. He also attempted to persuade corporations to keep American factories open or reopen factories that had closed.

His actions helped grow US manufacturing jobs. Unfortunately for some, many of the manufacturing jobs that were added were very different from the jobs that left.

# LOOK AT ME NOW

In a 2017 study, Manpower Group and UI Labs' Digital Manufacturing and Design Innovation Institute defined some roles manufacturers need to fill to succeed with the new digitally driven production processes.

- Digital manufacturing chief technology officer
- Digital manufacturing analyst
- Model-based systems engineer
- Manufacturing cybersecurity strategist
- Embedded product prognostics engineer
- Virtual reality/augmented reality system specialist
- Predictive maintenance system specialist
- Machine learning specialist
- Digital twin architect
- Predictive supply network engineer
- Supply network manager
- IT/OT systems engineer
- Digital manufacturing technical educator
- Digital factory automation engineer
- Collaborative robotics specialist
- Collaborative robotics technician
- Organizational management change strategist
- Worker experience designer
- User experience architect

The new jobs pay well above the average of all occupations, but also require advanced education or specialized training.

The United States lost some manufacturing jobs because corporations found cheaper labor elsewhere; technological change caused many lost opportunities, too. Automation, robotics, and other technologies have resulted in improved production and quality compared with human workers. And technology will continue to dominate and change future manufacturing processes.

An engineer jots down a detail on a project, sharing his work space with a mechanical arm. Human-machine collaboration in the coming years will become common in the manufacturing space.

## PREPPING FOR WORKPLACE TECH SUCCESS

Important traits for production workers in the twenty-first century include critical thinking, emotional intelligence, curiosity, creativity, adaptability, and resilience. Today's line workers also need computer literacy and proficiency in math, reading, and mechanical reasoning. Fortunately, high schoolers can get a head start on acquiring these skills.

Classes in math and English along with a heavy load of such science courses as physics, chemistry, physical science, materials science, green technology, and engineering help prepare the next generation's workforce. Art classes that include design and 3D modeling can also be helpful. Computer science that includes computer-assisted design (CAD), coding, and programming will help ready students for new technologies.

## MAY THE BEST ROBOT WIN

Extracurricular activities improve needed skills. For example, working on a robotics team offers practical, real-world experience. Teams participates in local, regional, national competitions, or international competitions.

For example, the annual international FIRST Robotics Competition brings together high school students at all skill levels. Teams have six weeks to raise money, brand themselves, and build and program industrial-size robots. The robots play games against robots from other teams, culminating in a championship event.

Adult coaches and mentors help students work as a team to practice engineering principles. Their goal is to increase students' interdisciplinary skills in science, technology, engineering, and mathematics.

FIRST is a nonprofit charity that seeks to inspire students' interest in education and careers in science and technology. It was founded in 1989 in Manchester, New Hampshire. According to the organization's website, the 2019 FIRST Robotics Competition involved 3,790 teams with more than 94,750 high school participants. It awarded more than $80 million in 2,000 individual college scholarships.

## FUN AND GAMES

Another robotics competition is the National Robotics Challenge in Marion, Ohio, which is open to students from sixth grade through graduate school. Founded in 1986 as the Society of Manufacturing Engineers Robotic Technology and Engineering Challenge, its purpose is to encourage future innovators and engineers. Rebranded as the National Robotics Challenge in 2004, the event offers twelve robotics contests, several related to manufacturing technologies:

- Autonomous Vehicle Challenge: To design and build a vehicle to complete an obstacle course.
- Interactivity Challenge: To simulate communication among computers, sensors, and microcontrollers.
- Internet of Things Challenge: To build a device that simulates communication, collection of data, and interactivity through a network.

Future factory workers, engineers, and manufacturers sometimes show some technical affinity at a young age, like these students working together to build a car in class.

- Manufacturing Workcell and Manufacturing Technology Development Challenge: To design, construct, and operate a system that performs one or more manufacturing processes.
- Pick and Place Programming Challenge: To program a robot to pick up objects and place them in specific locations, such as goods that would be moved in a factory warehouse.

# CHANGING MINDS

Despite the growing need for skilled production workers, many of today's students shun the idea of working in manufacturing. Perhaps they hold misconceptions about working in boring, repetitive jobs on dark, dirty factory floors. To dispel those thoughts and encourage the next generation to consider manufacturing careers, the Fabricators and Manufacturers Association, International designated the first Friday in October as Manufacturing Day in 2012.

In the now annual observance, manufacturers nationwide schedule open-door events to show potential workers what production in the twenty-first century is like: highly skilled workers operating in innovative work environments. The National Association of Manufacturers, the Manufacturing Institute, and the Hollings Manufacturing Extension Partnership also support the activities.

In 2015 and 2016, Deloitte Touche Tohmatsu Limited, commonly referred to as Deloitte, a multinational professional services network, measured the effects of Manufacturing Day. According to their reports, 81 percent of students who attended an event in 2015 became "more convinced that manufacturing provides careers that are interesting and rewarding." The number grew to 84 percent the next year. The results show a positive shift in students' attitudes toward the industry.

## CAMPING OUT

High schoolers, as well as students as young as seven, can gain hands-on experience for future manufacturing jobs at summer camps dedicated to technology. For example, iD Tech camps held at 150 universities worldwide help participants gain skills that are in demand. Topics offered include design, robotics, 3D printing, coding, programming, virtual reality, and artificial intelligence and machine learning.

Camps are available for all students, with some especially for teens and others designated "Girls Only." Its AcademyNEXT, for instance, is a three-week session for students ages sixteen to nineteen held at Stanford University in Stanford, California, and Rice University in Houston, Texas. Participants use data science, machine learning, and artificial intelligence as well as coding, robotics, and programming for team or individual projects. They also tour tech companies and present their projects to recruiters.

Computer camps focus on aspects of information technology. Education Unlimited, headquartered in Berkeley, California, offers students in grades one through twelve specialized camps across California and in the northeastern United States. Topics include coding, programming, graphic design, 3D imaging, and web design.

## DO IT YOURSELF

Fab Labs and makerspaces are community workshops where anyone can learn about and use the latest technology for making things. Products can be for personal use or prototypes of ideas for new products. Users share high-tech manufacturing machines that cut and bend a wide variety of materials. And almost anyone can use them to gain skills as well as create items.

Equipment at these workshops varies from place to place, but it usually includes 3D printers, laser cutters, milling machines, vinyl cutters, routers, and computers and monitors with supporting software, including computer-aided design. Users get hands-on experience with computer-controlled fabrication machines for their crafts and hobbies as well as potential employment opportunities.

These community workshops are usually supervised by a technician who acts as a teacher or guide. He or she usually has a mechanical or electrical engineering or manufacturing background or electronics and programming skills. The technician's job is to maintain the equipment and supplies as well

Many tech-inclined teens love to take apart common household items and reassemble them for fun. Such tinkering is a good hobby for students who one day plan to work with machines somehow.

as train participants on the available software and machinery.

Fab Labs and makerspaces are found in high schools, colleges, libraries, and community centers on every continent, in bustling urban communities and remote villages. To find one near you, enter "Fab Lab" or "makerspace" and your city or county in the web browser. For a list of member Fab Labs, contact the Fab Lab Foundation.

## MANUFACTURING SCHOOLS

Manufacturing schools are trade schools dedicated to specific training for the production workforce. For example, the Precision Manufacturing Institute in Meadville, Pennsylvania, offers instruction in machining, arc welding and electromechanical technology toward diploma programs for CNC machinists, CNC operators, electric arc welding, and electromechanical technology. CNC machinists and operators work with precision computer numeric controlled (CNC) machinery to cut, grind, or drill metal, plastic, or other material to produce parts and tools. CNC operators feed material into the machines, check quality, and maintain the machinery.

The school is licensed and accredited by the Pennsylvania State Board of Private Licensed Schools and the Accrediting Commission of Career Schools and Colleges and approved by the US Department of Education.

Most trade schools offer diplomas or certifications. Some also award associate's and bachelor's degrees.

Goodwin College offers career-focused programs tailored to employers' in-demand skills with year-round classes days, evenings, and weekends as well as online. Among other areas of study, the school offers certificates in CNC machining, metrology, and manufacturing technology; CNC machining; and welding.

It also has associate's degree in science programs for CNC machining; quality management systems; and supply chain and logistics management, as well as a bachelor's of science degree in manufacturing management. The school is accredited by the New England Commission of Higher Education and the Board of Governors for Higher Education of the State of Connecticut.

Community colleges and traditional four-year colleges and universities are also responding to the need for education in manufacturing technology by offering degree programs and certifications in a wide variety of production-job-related courses and majors.

Because of the serious shortage of skilled workers to fill job openings, some manufacturers may hire workers and provide on-the-job training. However, preparing prior to applying for a job increases the chances of getting hired and enjoying a successful career.

**ADDITIVE MANUFACTURING** A production process that creates a physical object by adding thin layers of material according to a plan that uses computer-aided design software; also called 3D printing.

**ARTIFICIAL INTELLIGENCE** A branch of computer science that lets machines work and react like humans.

**ASSEMBLY LINE** A step-by-step manufacturing method where workers and machines complete a sequence of simple steps toward the creation of a final product; sometimes called a production line.

**CLOUD COMPUTING** The use of remote servers to store, manage, and process data on an internet network instead of a personal computer or a company's on-site system.

**COBOT** A cooperative robot designed to work alongside humans.

**DIVISION OF LABOR** The practice of assigning each worker a single task in the manufacturing process, instead of a single craftsman making an entire item.

**E-LEARNING** Lessons available through electronic media, often online.

**END EFFECTOR** The object at the end of a robotic arm that performs desired tasks.

**FLOW PRODUCTION** A manufacturing process using interchangeable parts with a moving conveyor system.

**GEOSYNCHRONOUS EARTH ORBIT (GEO) SATELLITE** A satellite that stays in one place in space in relation to Earth's rotation.

**GREEN MANUFACTURING** Production methods that use environmentally friendly practices.

**INFORMATION TECHNOLOGY** Software that enables computers to save, recall, send, and manipulate data.

**INTERCHANGEABLE PARTS** Parts of an item designed to work in all products of the same kind.

**IOT PLATFORM** The bridge between the IoT devices that collect information and the data network where it will be stored, managed, and processed.

**KILN** An oven used to fire pottery to make it stronger and more durable.

**LEAN MANUFACTURING** Production methods that reduce wasted time as well as materials.

**LINE WORKER** An employee who works on an assembly line.

**MANUFACTURING** The process of making items for parts or complete products for sale to end users.

**MANUFACTURING EXECUTION SYSTEM (MES)** Software that controls the activities on the factory floor, including scheduling, maintenance, and quality control.

**OPERATIONAL TECHNOLOGY** Hardware and software that controls or monitors automation machinery.

**RECYCLED PULP** A material made from paper fibers from recycled paper that has had ink removed.

**SUSTAINABLE FACTORY** A manufacturing plant that can run for more than a century with very little enviromental impact.

Association for Manufacturing Technology (AMT)
7901 Jones Branch Drive, Suite 900
McLean, VA 22102-3316
(703) 893-2900
Website: https://www.amtonline.org
Twitter: @amtonline
The Association for Manufacturing Technology represents
   builders and distributors of manufacturing technology.
   Its International Manufacturing Technology Show,
   held in North America, offers displays of the latest
   innovations. The association also provides member
   businesses with programs and services to increase sales
   and lower costs.

BC Alliance for Manufacturing
10451 Shellbridge Way, Suite 230
Richmond BC V6X 2W9
Canada
(604) 900-1980
Website: https://www.manufacturingbc.org
The BC Alliance for Manufacturing is a group of
   manufacturing associations that promotes manufacturing
   in British Columbia. Membership includes businesses in
   design, materials, and fabrication as well as organizations
   that train workers and chambers of commerce.

Canadian Council of Technicians & Technologists (CCTT)
2197 Riverside Drive, Suite 301
Ottawa, ON K1H 7X3

Canada
(613) 238-8123
Website: http://www.cctt.ca
CCTT accredits certification programs that train technicians
    and technologists to work with new technologies in
    Canada. It represents students and graduates of applied
    science and engineering technology subjects.

Fabricators & Manufacturers Association,
    International (FMA)
2135 Point Boulevard
Elgin, IL 60123
(815) 399-8700
Website: http://fmanet.org
Twitter: @FMAmembership
Members of the Fabricators & Manufacturers Association,
    International include workers in North American processing,
    forming, and fabricating positions. Their mission is to
    encourage the growth and sustainability of those industries.

Manufacturing Enterprise Solutions Association International
107 S. Southgate Drive
Chandler, AZ 85226
(480) 893-6883
Website: http://mesa.org
Twitter: @MESAp2e
MESA International members include manufacturing
    companies, information technology suppliers and
    workers, and educators of students dedicated to
    helping manufacturers improve their operations using
    information technology.

National Association of Manufacturers
733 10th Street NW, Suite 700
Washington, DC 20001
(800) 814-8468
Website: http://www.nam.org
Facebook: @NAMpage
Twitter: @ShopFloorNAM
YouTube: NAMvideo
The National Association of Manufacturers focuses on
    developing tomorrow's manufacturing workforce. It
    represents manufacturers in all fifty states and advocates
    for a favorable US policy for manufacturing.

National Council for Advanced Manufacturing (NACFAM)
2025 M Street, NW, Suite 800
Washington, DC 20036
(202) 367-1247
Website: http://www.nacfam.org
NACFAM advocates for US manufacturing policy to
    encourage technological innovation, supply chain
    integration, sustainable manufacturing, and workforce
    development. Its members include corporations, trade
    associations, and nonprofit groups dedicated to improving
    the US economy through strong advanced manufacturing.

Asimov, Isaac. I, *Robot*. New York, NY: Bantam Dell, 2004.

Bunz, Mercedes, and Graham Meikle. *The Internet of Things*. Cambridge, UK: Polity Press, 2018.

Ceceri, Kathy. *Making Simple Robots: Exploring Cutting-Edge Robotics with Everyday Stuff*. San Francisco, CA: Maker Media, 2015.

Dennis, Pascal. *Lean Production Simplified*. Boca Raton, FL: CRC Press, 2015.

Horne, Richard, and Kirk Hausman Kalani. *3D Printing for Dummies*. Hoboken, NJ: John Wiley & Sons Inc., 2019.

Husain, Amir. *The Sentient Machine: The Coming Age of Artificial Intelligence*. New York, NY: Scribner, 2017.

Isogawa, Yoshihito. *The LEGO BOOST Idea Book: 95 Simple Robots and Hints for Making More!* San Francisco, CA: Apress, 2018.

Kloski, Liza Wallach, and Nick Kloski. *Getting Started with 3D Printing: A Hands-on Guide to the Hardware, Software, and Services That Make the 3D Printing Ecosystem*. San Francisco, CA: Maker Media, 2019.

Miller, Michael. *Internet of Things*. London, UK: Pearson Education, 2015.

Mueller, John, and Luca Massaron. *Artificial Intelligence For Dummies*. Hoboken, NJ: John Wiley & Sons Inc., 2018.

Papagiannis, Helen. *Augmented Human: How Technology Is Shaping the New Reality*. Sebastopol, CA: O'Reilly Media Inc., 2017.

Tegmark, Max. *Life 3.0: Being Human in the Age of Artificial Intelligence*. New York, NY: Vintage, 2018.

# BIBLIOGRAPHY

3DPI. "The Free Beginner's Guide. 3DPrintingIndustry.com, Retrieved December 28, 2018. https://3dprintingindustry .com/3d-printing-basics-free-beginners-guide.

Budiac, Jeff. "The Manufacturing Jobs of the Future." Softwareconnect.com, January 11, 2018. https:// softwareconnect.com/manufacturing/jobs-of-the-future.

Columbus, Louis. "10 Ways Cloud Computing Will Drive Manufacturing Growth in 2018." Manufacturing.net, February 23, 2018. https://www.manufacturing.net /article/2018/02/10-ways-cloud-computing-will-drive -manufacturing-growth-2018.

DeVore, Chuck. "312,000 Jobs Added in December, Manufacturing Growing 714% Faster Under Trump than Obama." Forbes, January 4, 2019. https://www.forbes.com /sites/chuckdevore/2019/01/04/312000-jobs-added -in-december-manufacturing-growing-714-faster-under -trump-than-obama/#77205c635b50.

Forrest, Conner. "Chinese factory Replaces 90% of Humans with Robots, Production Soars." TechRepublic.com, July 30, 2015. https://www.techrepublic.com/article/chinese -factory-replaces-90-of-humans-with-robots-production -soars.

Hamner, Burt. "Technology, Pollution Prevention." PollutionIssues.com, retrieved January 22, 2019. http:// www.pollutionissues.com/Te-Un/Technology-Pollution -Prevention.html.

History. "This Day in History December 1, 1913: Ford's Assembly Line Starts Rolling." November 13, 2009. https:// www.history.com/this-day-in-history/fords-assembly-line -starts-rolling.

Lewis, Michael R. "What Is Nanotechnology—Examples, Future Applications & Risks." MoneyCrashers.com, January 2, 2019. https://www.moneycrashers.com /nanotechnology-examples-future-applications-risks.

Long, Heather. "U.S. Has Lost 5 million Manufacturing Jobs Since 2000." CNN.com, March 26, 2016. https://money .cnn.com/2016/03/29/news/economy/us-manufacturing -jobs/index.html.

Matthews, Kayla. "5 Manufacturing Applications for Robotics in 2018." Manufacturing.net, February 28, 2018. https:// www.manufacturing.net/articls/2018/02/5-manufacturing -applications-robotics-2018.

ME Mechanical Team. "Manufacturing Process." ME-MechanicalEngineering.com, April 23, 2016. https://me -mechanicalengineering.com/historical-development-of -materials-and-manufacturing-process.

National Association of Manufacturers. "20 Facts About Manufacturing." Retrieved July 17, 2019. https://www.nam .org/facts-about-manufacturing.

Tang, Cindy. "The Terracotta Army—Why and How They Were Made." China Highlights.com, March 1, 2019. https://www.chinahighlights.com/xian/terracotta-army.

Urquhart, Kristina. "Universally Speaking: Universal Robots' CEO on the Future of Cobots." AutomationMag.com, January 23, 2019. https://www.automationmag.com /technology/robotics/8976-universally-speaking -universal-robots-and-the-future-of-cobots.

Wright, Ian. "What Can Augmented Reality Do for Manufacturing?" Engineering.com, May 11, 2017. https:// www.engineering.com/AdvancedManufacturing /ArticleID/14904/What-Can-Augmented-Reality-Do-for -Manufacturing.aspx.

# INDEX

## ABOUT THE AUTHOR

Mary-Lane Kamberg is a professional writer specializing in nonfiction for young readers. She is the author of the following Rosen Publishing titles: *Working as a Plumber, Pipefitter, and Steamfitter, Drones and Commerce, Getting a Job in the IT Industry, Working as a Mechanic in Your Community,* and *How Business Decisions Are Made.* She lives in Olathe, Kansas, and serves as coleader of the Kansas City Writers Group.

## PHOTO CREDITS

Cover baranozdemir/E+/Getty Images; p. 6 Maxim Kalmykov/ Shutterstock.com; p. 9 De Agostini Picture Library/Getty Images; p. 12 Schenectady Museum Association/Corbis Historical/Getty Images; p. 16 Heritage Images/Hulton Archive/Getty Images; p. 19 Chan Looi Tat/AFP/Getty Images; p. 22 South China Morning Post/Getty Images; p. 25 Vittoriano Rastelli/Corbis Historical/ Getty Images; p. 27 Westend61/Getty Images; p. 30 Moreno Soppelsa/Shutterstock.com; p. 35 Tyler Olson/Shutterstock.com; p. 37 Frank Micelotta Archive/Getty Images; p. 40 Photo 12/ Alamy Stock Photo; p. 44 © iStockphoto.com/fmajor; pp. 47, 56 wavebreakmedia/Shutterstock.com; p. 50 Kampan/Shutterstock.com; p. 53 Jonutis/Shutterstock.com; p. 59 Jacob Boomsma/Shutterstock .com; p. 61 Suwin/Shutterstock.com; p. 64 Monkey Business Images/Shutterstock.com; p. 67 Lightfield Studios/Shutterstock .com.

Design and Layout: Nicole Russo-Duca; Photo Researcher: Sherri Jackson